Why Don't Sharks Have BONES?

This edition published in 2022 by Arcturus Publishing Limited
26/27 Bickels Yard, 151–153 Bermondsey Street,
London SE1 3HA

Illustrator: Luke Séguin-Magee
Authors: Clare Hibbert, William Potter, and Marc Powell
Editors: Susie Rae and Joe Harris
Designer: Rosie Bellwood

CH007051NT
Supplier: 10, Date 0122, Print run 001

Printed in the UK

CONTENTS

ARE YOU READY TO MAKE A SPLASH?

Then zip up your wet suit and strap on your scuba tank for a deep dive into the wet and wonderful world of undersea creatures.

You'll meet the biggest creature that ever lived on our planet, speedy sharks, venomous jellyfish, exploding crustaceans, the fierce, fanged monsters that live miles down in the dark depths, and much, much more!

COOL CETACEANS

WHAT'S A CETACEAN?

Cetaceans are aquatic mammals that include toothed whales—such as sperm whales, orcas, narwhals, and dolphins—and baleen whales, like the blue whale, right whale, and bowhead.

WHAT IS THE LARGEST ANIMAL IN THE WORLD...EVER?

The blue whale is the largest creature known to have lived on our planet—bigger than any dinosaur. The longest blue whale ever found measured just over 33m (110ft). That's the length of nine family cars end to end!

HOW HEAVY IS A BLUE WHALE?

A blue whale can weigh up to 125 metric tons (250,000lbs). That's as much as 23 elephants, 230 cows, or 1,800 adult men.

HOW HEAVY IS A BLUE WHALE'S TONGUE?

A blue whale's tongue can weigh the same as an elephant.

DID YOU KNOW?

A baby blue whale drinks 0.28 metric tons (60 gallons) of milk from its mother every day.

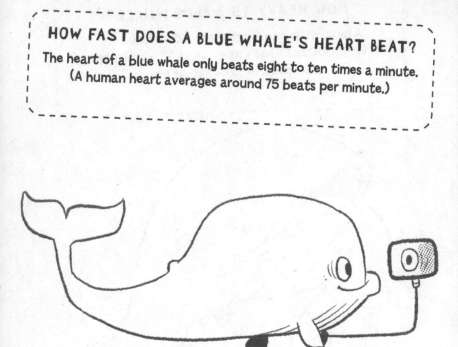

HOW DOES A WHALE SEE WHAT'S BEHIND IT?

Whales can't actually move their eyeballs. In order to see behind, a whale has to move its entire body.

HOW DEEP DO WHALES DIVE?

A sperm whale can dive to depths of 2km (1.25 miles).

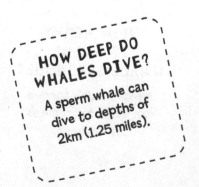

WHY ARE WHALES SO CRUSTY?

Because whales are so slow-moving, barnacles often get attached to them. They can comfortably carry up to 454kg (1,000lb) of barnacles around with them!

HOW FAR DOES A WHALE NOISE TRAVEL?

Using sonar equipment, scientists can detect the sounds made by fin whales and blue whales from up to 850km (528 miles) away.

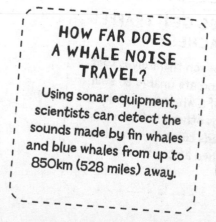

HOW DO YOU MAKE A SHARK EXPLODE?

Killer whales have been known to attack sharks by launching themselves into their prey's stomach like a torpedo. The force of the impact can cause the shark to explode.

ARE SOME WHALES TOOTHLESS?

Yes. Whales without teeth are called baleen whales. Blue whales, humpback whales, right whales, and gray (sometimes spelled grey) whales are all baleen whales. They have bristly baleen instead of teeth, which they use to "'sieve" food from the water.

WHY DO WHALES GET TRAPPED ON BEACHES?

Whales sometimes beach themselves (get stranded on land) and are unable to swim back into the sea. If a whale is stranded, its distress call brings other whales to help, which sometimes leads to whole schools of whales being beached at the same time.

ARE DOLPHINS WHALES?

Yes. The two main types of whale are whales with teeth and whales without teeth. Dolphins are toothed whales. Other toothed whales include sperm whales and belugas. Orcas, also known as killer whales, are a type of dolphin.

HOW MANY TYPES OF DOLPHIN ARE THERE?

Experts cannot agree on an exact figure, but there are about 40. One problem is that not everyone agrees on which species are dolphins. Another is that some kinds are rare and are dying out.

WHAT ARE PORPOISES?

Porpoises are the smallest members of the whale family. They are only 1.5-2.5m (5-8ft) long. The harbor (or harbour) porpoise is the best known. It is found in cool, coastal waters all over the northern hemisphere.

DID YOU KNOW?

If a dolphin loses its tail, scientists can attach an artificial rubber tail made from the same material used to make Formula 1 car tires. It's proven to work as well as the real thing!

WHICH ANIMALS EAT DOLPHINS?

Sharks eat dolphins. Many dolphins have shark-bite scars on their bodies, so at least some of them get away. Orcas eat dolphins too—even though they belong to the same family.

HOW MANY TEETH DO DOLPHINS HAVE?

Dolphins have wide, cone-shaped teeth, just right for grasping slippery prey. One set of between 60 and 100 teeth lasts them a lifetime. The teeth start coming through when baby dolphins are about five weeks old.

HOW DO DOLPHINS FIND FOOD?

Dolphins make high-pitched clicks that travel through the water. The clicking sounds bounce off objects, sending echoes back to the dolphins. This is called echolocation. As they receive the echoes of the clicks, dolphins can build a detailed picture of what is in the water. They can tell the exact shape and structure of things and how far away they are.

DOES A DOLPHIN HAVE A MELON IN ITS HEAD?

A dolphin's bulging forehead is a vital part of its echolocation equipment. The bulge is a fatty organ called the "melon." Its job is to precisely direct or point the dolphin's clicks so that picture it builds is as accurate as possible.

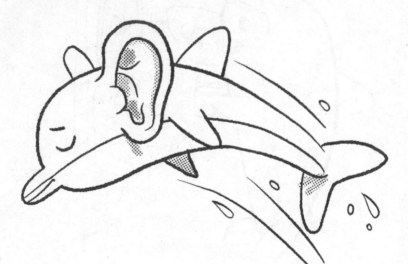

DO DOLPHINS HAVE EARS?

Dolphins have internal ears. Some sounds reach dolphin ears through small openings just behind each eye. Most sounds, however, reach their ears by vibrating, or wobbling, along their lower jaws.

HOW DO DOLPHINS SLEEP?

Dolphins sleep with one eye open! They shut down each side of their brain separately to rest.

DID YOU KNOW?

Fishing nets are designed with holes in the bottom to let dolphins and other big creatures escape. The nets work because fish, such as haddock, are not brainy enough to realize they can swim downward!

DO DOLPHINS CRY?

Yes, dolphins' eyes "weep" all the time. The oily tears keep their eyes clean—they're not a sign that dolphins feel sad!

ARE DOLPHINS FUSSY EATERS?

Dolphins have taste buds at the base of their tongue. Experts are still investigating dolphins' sense of taste, and we do not know very much about it. However, dolphins appear to prefer certain foods to others.

WHAT'S A BAIT BALL?

Dolphins have some cunning hunting methods. They often team up to drive fish into a ball shape called a bait ball. Other tricks include whacking fish with their tails to stun them or herding fish into the shallows.

ARE DOLPHINS BIRDWATCHERS?

Dolphins often poke their heads above the surface to look around. This is called spy-hopping. They look out for big crowds of seabirds—a clue that there'll be plenty of fish in the water below.

HOW FRIENDLY ARE DOLPHINS?

Dolphins are very sociable and live in groups called pods. They touch each other when they are being friendly. They pat, stroke, and nuzzle their friends with their flippers and snouts.

CAN DOLPHINS SMELL?

Dolphins have no olfactory (smelling) nerves, so they cannot smell at all. However, they can detect chemicals in the water using their taste buds.

CAN FLIPPERS BE USED LIKE HANDS?

Dolphins have extra touch receptors on their flippers, so these are more sensitive than other parts of their bodies. Dolphins sometimes use their flippers to feel for crustaceans hidden in the sand of the seabed.

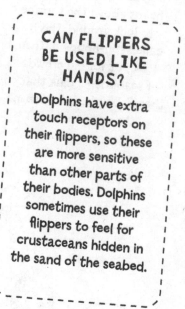

CAN DOLPHINS USE A MIRROR?

Dolphins can recognize their own reflections in a mirror. Only a few other animals—including humans, chimpanzees, and magpies—can do this.

CAN DOLPHINS TALK?

Dolphins make all sorts of sounds when they are "talking" to each other—squawks, whistles, squeaks, barks, groans, and moans. Experts have even noticed that each dolphin group or pod has its own way of talking, like a "dialect."

CAN WE TALK WITH DOLPHINS?

Humans are the only animals that use spoken language. However, researchers have shown that dolphins can be taught to understand sound-based language and sign language. They can even grasp how changing the order of words changes their meaning.

HOW ELSE CAN DOLPHINS COMMUNICATE?

Dolphins use body language to communicate too. A dolphin might roll over and "play dead" to show that it is no threat to another dolphin. Or it may shake its head rapidly from side to side as a sign of aggression.

DO DOLPHINS HAVE NAMES?

Dolphins often "call out" the signature whistles of other dolphins. They are using the sounds like names to call their friends!

CAN DOLPHINS SMILE?

One reason why people find dolphins so appealing may be their "smile." It's not a real smile, though—it's just the way dolphins' mouths are structured.

DO ALL DOLPHINS LIVE IN GROUPS?

It's unusual for dolphins to live alone. Sometimes lone dolphins show up near shores and choose to live near humans. It may be that they've become separated from their pod, or they are too old to keep up.

WHAT IS A POD?

Different dolphin species group together in different kinds of pods. Bottlenose dolphins often form groups of only females, or only females and calves. Dusky dolphins and white-beaked dolphins prefer to live in mixed pods that contain males, females, and calves.

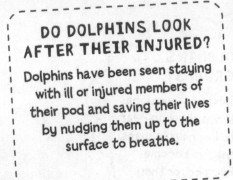

DO DOLPHINS LOOK AFTER THEIR INJURED?

Dolphins have been seen staying with ill or injured members of their pod and saving their lives by nudging them up to the surface to breathe.

DO DOLPHINS EVER FIGHT EACH OTHER?

Yes. They're not always friendly! Male dolphins will fight rivals to win a mate—they fight by bashing each other with their tails.

ARE DOLPHINS CAMOUFLAGED?

Dolphins have a special kind of camouflage that makes them perfectly adapted to their watery habitat. Viewed from above, their darker backs are hard to spot against the watery depths. Viewed from below, their paler undersides blend in with the sunlit surface.

HOW FAST CAN DOLPHINS SWIM?

Dolphins cruise along at 11-12km/h (7-8mph), but speed up to chase prey. Orcas can swim at 48km/h (30mph) in short bursts.

HOW FAR DO DOLPHINS SWIM?

Dolphins stick to their home ranges. Ocean species that live far away from the shore have the largest ranges, because their food is more spread out. For example, dusky dolphins range over 1,500 square km (580 square miles).

DO DOLPHINS MIGRATE?

Not really, though they might move into slightly warmer waters as the seasons change. They don't make regular long journeys like some of their whale cousins do.

DO DOLPHINS LIVE IN RIVERS?

Several kinds of dolphin live in rivers. South America's great Amazon River is home to two types—tucuxi and botos. Many river dolphins are endangered. The Yangtze river dolphin recently became extinct because of pollution.

WHAT ARE BLOWHOLES USED FOR?

Dolphins come up to the surface to breathe. They take in air and get rid of waste gas through their blowhole, a hole on the top of their head. When dolphins are underwater, a flap covers the blowhole so water can't get in. Dolphins and other toothed whales have one blowhole. The prize for the most impressive blowhole goes to the blue whale. Its blowhole sprays the water sitting on top of it up to 12m (40ft) high.

HOW LONG CAN DOLPHINS STAY UNDERWATER?

It depends on the species and their age (older dolphins have bigger lungs). The longest is about 15 minutes. Dolphins slow down their heartbeat during a dive to reduce how much oxygen they use up.

HOW MANY YOUNG DO DOLPHINS HAVE?

Most dolphin mothers give birth to a single calf—twins are very rare. The calf is born tail first and can swim right away. Its mother nudges it toward the surface to take its very first breath.

DO DOLPHINS HAVE BABYSITTERS?

Any adult in the dolphin pod will care for or discipline the calves. Female "aunts" babysit while the mothers hunt. Youngsters that don't come when they're called or misbehave in some other way are scolded with a tail slap.

HOW LONG DO DOLPHIN CALVES STAY WITH THEIR MOTHER?

Calves stick with their mamas for at least two to three years, and sometimes for as long as six years.

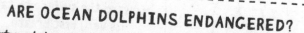

ARE OCEAN DOLPHINS ENDANGERED?

Unfortunately, some human activities harm dolphins. Dolphins can get trapped in large fishing nets. Many, including the rare humpback dolphin, are threatened because of pollution, which damages their habitat and the fish they eat.

SUPER SHARKS

HOW BIG DO GREAT WHITE SHARKS GET?

Great white sharks can grow up to 6.1m (20ft) long. Females are, on average, about 1m (3ft) longer than males.

DID YOU KNOW?

Great white sharks have a bite three times more powerful than that of an African lion.

WHY SHOULD YOU NEVER FLIP A SHARK?

If a shark gets turned on to its back, it goes into a state of paralysis for up to 15 minutes.

WHY DO SHARKS HAVE TO KEEP SWIMMING?

Some breeds of shark will drown if they stop swimming. They have to keep water moving through their gills at all times, so they can never really sleep.

WHAT IS THE MOST COMMON SHARK?

There are over 500 species, or types, of shark. Sharks come in many shapes and sizes. Dogfish are the most common ones. They are about 1m (3ft) long.

DO SHARKS SLEEP?

Sharks never fall deeply asleep like humans. They keep swimming to move water through their gills. They have "resting times," though, when they let one half of their brain turn off.

WHERE DO SHARKS LIVE?

Sharks live in all the world's oceans, from icy polar waters to warm, tropical seas. They also live at all levels of the ocean, from the shallows to the deep.

DO SHARKS LIVE IN RIVERS?

Bull sharks swim far up rivers and into lakes, so they are more likely to meet (and eat) bathers and swimmers than sharks that stay out at sea. Bull sharks are widespread and found in the Amazon, Zambezi, and Ganges Rivers.

HOW MANY TEETH DO SHARKS HAVE?

Sharks' teeth are replaced every couple of weeks, so they are always in peak condition. They are arranged in rows in the mouth. As one tooth or row of teeth falls out, new ones move forward to take their place. Over their lifetime, sharks may go through 20,000 teeth!

ARE ALL SHARK TEETH THE SAME?

Shark teeth come in different shapes, to suit their owners' diets. Spear-like teeth are good for catching slippery fish and squid, while blunt teeth can crush shells. Great whites have triangular cutting teeth for slicing into seals.

IS THERE REALLY A COOKIECUTTER SHARK?

Yes. The cookiecutter shark is named for its unusual feeding
method. It bites circular chunks out of larger animals, such as
dolphins and whales. The wounds eventually heal, leaving the
victims with 5-cm (2-in) round scars.

HOW DO SHARKS BREATHE?

Like all fish, sharks take in oxygen from the water. As a shark swims, it gulps in seawater and pushes it out through gill slits on the sides of its head. Inside the gills, oxygen passes from the water into the shark's bloodstream.

DID YOU KNOW?

Sharks will eat anything, even parts of their own bodies that have been bitten after an attack by another animal.

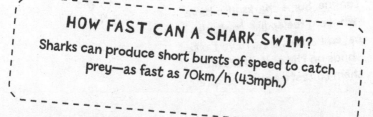

HOW FAST CAN A SHARK SWIM?

Sharks can produce short bursts of speed to catch prey—as fast as 70km/h (43mph.)

Sharks need to eat around three percent of their body weight in food each day just to survive.

DID YOU KNOW?

Little is known about the megamouth shark as it was first discovered by scientists in 1976. Only three photographs of it in its natural habitat exist in the entire world.

DO SHARKS HAVE TASTE BUDS?

Sharks have taste buds all over the inside of their mouth and throat, not just on the tongue. Some sharks also have whiskery feeler-like tentacles called barbels that have taste buds on the ends that allow them to taste and "feel" prey.

DO SHARKS GIVE BIRTH TO LIVE YOUNG?

Lemon sharks are one of the few shark species that give birth to live young. Their litters can contain up to 17 pups. The pups develop inside their mother, and an umbilical cord brings them oxygen and nutrients.

DO SHARK MOTHERS LOOK AFTER THEIR BABIES?

Shark mothers abandon their babies, but they give them a good start in life. They have their pups in shallow, coastal waters, where they will be safe during their early years.

WHAT DOES A BABY SHARK LOOK LIKE?

Most sharks develop inside eggs inside their mother's body, not connected to her by an umbilical cord or placenta. When they are fully developed, the babies "hatch" and are born. Sometimes the newborn pups are still attached to their yolk sac, which provides them with food.

WHY IS IT BAD NEWS TO BE A SHARK TWIN?

A female tiger shark carries several babies during pregnancy but only gives birth to one. In the womb, the strongest baby eats the others until it is the only one left.

WHAT IS THE BIGGEST FISH IN THE WORLD?

The whale shark is the largest fish alive, growing to around 18m (59ft) long.

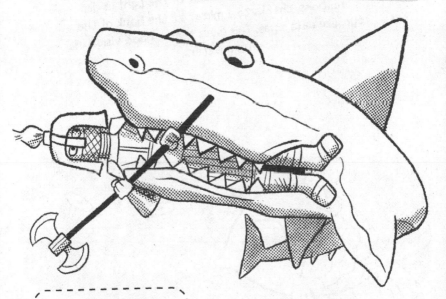

DO SHARKS CLOSE THEIR EYES WHEN THEY BITE?

Some sharks have a third eyelid that draws across the eye to protect it when the shark bites. Others simply roll their eyeballs up at the moment of biting.

DID YOU KNOW?

Some of the items found inside sharks' stomachs include a horse's head, a porcupine, parts of bicycles and cars, a sheep, a chicken coop—and even a suit of armor with the remains of a French soldier inside!

CAN SHARKS SEE IN THE DARK?

Unlike other fish, sharks can dilate (widen) their pupils to control how much light enters the eye. They can also make the most of the light in dim conditions, thanks to a mirror at the back of the eye, like cats' eyes. This gives sharks good vision in murky waters.

WHY ARE SOME SHARKS BLIND?

Most Greenland sharks are blinded by parasites called copepods that fix themselves to the sharks' eyes. However, the copepods produce light that attracts prey, so it doesn't really matter that the sharks can't see!

WHAT'S SPECIAL ABOUT A SHARK'S NOSE?

Sharks have special organs in their snouts that detect the electric fields produced by other living creatures.

DID YOU KNOW?

The washed-up, empty egg case of a dogfish, skate, or shark is called a mermaid's purse. The egg cases harden in the water and protect the growing embryo for six to 12 months. Then, the pup swims out of the case.

DO SHARKS SEE IN BLACK AND WHITE?

Not all sharks' eyes are the same, but most only see the world in monochrome (black and white).

WHAT DO SHARKS FEEL LIKE?

A shark's skin is covered in sharp, tooth-like scales called denticles, which feel like sandpaper. The denticles reduce drag. Throughout the shark's life, old denticles drop off and are replaced by new ones.

ARE MOST SHARKS DANGEROUS?

Even though there are more than 500 known species of shark in the world, only about 12 are actually dangerous to humans. Most attacks are accidents when a shark mistakes a human for another animal.

WHY DON'T SHARKS HAVE BONES?

For millions of years sharks have developed separately from bony fish. They grew skeletons made of cartilage rather than bone. Cartilage is the same material that holds our ears and noses in shape. It is lighter and more flexible than bones, giving sharks the ability to move in a quick and fluid way.

DID YOU KNOW?

While most fish use gas-filled swim bladders for buoyancy (staying afloat), a shark uses its liver for the same purpose.

HOW GOOD IS SHARK HEARING?

Sharks can pick up low-frequency sounds best and are more likely to react to irregular sounds—the sorts of sounds produced by an injured animal thrashing about. Sound is often the first thing that alerts sharks to prey.

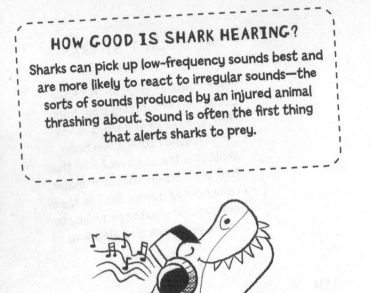

HOW GOOD IS A SHARK'S SENSE OF SMELL?

Sharks use smell to find a mate and to navigate, but most of all to track down prey. They show interest in certain smells—such as blood—and totally ignore others.

HOW DOES A SHARK SMELL?

As a shark swims, seawater flows through its nostrils—the two flaps of skin at the end of its snout—and on to the nasal sacs behind. These sacs have sensory cells that can detect scents and send messages to the shark's brain.

ARE SHARKS REALLY SENSITIVE TO BLOOD?

They can't distinguish between as many different smells as we can, but they are very sensitive to certain smells. They can sense one drop of blood in a million drops of water, or a small amount of blood in water over 0.4km (quarter of a mile) away.

WHAT IS A LATERAL LINE?

Sharks have a line of sensory cells running along each side of their head and body. Water swishes over these lines of cells as sharks swim, sending signals to their brain about pressure changes and movement in the water.

WHAT DOES A LATERAL LINE DO?

The lateral line allows sharks to build up a clear "picture" of their surroundings—and to notice changes to the usual currents. Sharks can pick up the vibrations produced by a thrashing fish from 100m (328ft) away!

DO SHARKS HAVE A SIXTH SENSE?

Sharks have small pits, or openings, around their nose called ampullae of Lorenzini. These can sense electrical signals from about 50cm (20in) away. Moving muscles produce electricity, so this sense helps sharks target their prey even more precisely.

DID YOU KNOW?

In an effort to get them to mate, a German aquarium plays love songs to its sharks!

ARE SHARKS THE ONLY ANIMALS THAT SENSE ELECTRICAL SIGNALS?

No. Their close cousins, rays, have this ability too, and so do some other aquatic animals, including electric eels, some dolphins, and platypuses.

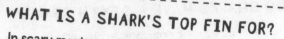

WHAT IS A SHARK'S TOP FIN FOR?

In scary movies, a dorsal fin poking above the surface warns us that a shark is coming. In reality, the dorsal fin acts like a stabilizer and stops the shark from rolling in the water.

WHY DOESN'T A SHARK SINK?

The flow of water over sharks' pectoral (side) and pelvic (bottom) fins produces lift—just like air flowing over a plane's wing. This stops sharks from sinking. Sharks change direction by tilting their fins.

WHICH SHARK HAS A TAIL AS LONG AS ITS BODY?

The thresher shark has a tail fin that can be 3m (10ft) long, as long as its body. The shark is thought to use its tail to whip and stun prey that it then turns upon to eat.

DID YOU KNOW?

A whale shark can filter up to 1,800 metric tons (400,000 gallons) of water an hour when feeding.

DID YOU KNOW?

Some sharks can detect the smell of fish at concentrations as low as one part in ten billion.

DO SOME SHARKS REST ON THE SEA BED?

Sharks that spend most of their time on the sea bed do not need to use their fins for bursts of speed. Nurse sharks' tails have almost no bottom lobe on their tail fins. These sharks sweep their eel-like tails to and fro as they hunt for crabs and lobsters.

HOW DO SHARKS FIND THEIR WAY?

Their electrosensory perception helps them to use the Earth's magnetism like an in-built compass.

HOW DO GREAT WHITE SHARKS HUNT?

The great white's hunting method helps it kill seals without injuring itself. First, it rises up at an angle and takes a surprise bite out of its prey. Then it circles, waiting for blood loss to weaken its victim, before moving in to enjoy its meal.

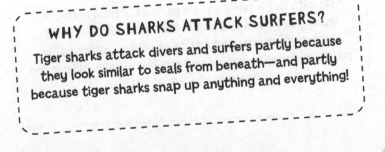

WHY DO SHARKS ATTACK SURFERS?

Tiger sharks attack divers and surfers partly because they look similar to seals from beneath—and partly because tiger sharks snap up anything and everything!

HOW LIKELY ARE YOU TO BE KILLED BY A SHARK?

There are fewer than 100 shark attacks per year and only 5 to 15 fatalities. You are 250 times more likely to be killed by lightning than by a shark.

CAN SHARKS HAVE BABIES ON THEIR OWN?

Despite not having a male partner, a hammerhead shark gave birth in a zoo in Nebraska, USA, in 2001. The female shark used a type of reproduction called parthenogenesis in order to keep the species alive when no male sharks are available.

DO SHARKS HUNT IN TEAMS?

Copper sharks and silky sharks co-operate to hunt. They work together to herd fish into a ball shape called a bait ball. Then the sharks start snapping at the closely packed fish. Gray (or grey) nurse sharks work together, too. They thrash their tails to drive fish into the shallows. The action creates underwater waves that sweep the prey toward shore. Reef sharks may follow the nurse sharks to steal a share of the trapped fish.

WHAT ARE "WOLVES OF THE SEA"?

Blue sharks are sometimes called the "wolves of the sea." They spend a lot of their time as loners, but they also form schools, or groups, when they hunt. Blue sharks eat fish, squid, and seabirds.

WHAT IS A FEEDING FRENZY?

Once a group of sharks finds lots of prey, the blood in the water and the jerky movements of the fish overexcite the sharks. They might lunge at each other as well as the prey!

WHY DO BASKING SHARKS SWIM WITH THEIR MOUTHS WIDE OPEN?

Filter feeders, such as basking sharks, swim along with their huge mouths wide open. Every so often they shut their jaws, forcing seawater through the gills. Bristles called gill rakers strain food from the water and channel it into the throat.

HOW DO MEGAMOUTHS FIND THEIR FOOD?

Megamouths are mysterious sharks that live in the deep ocean. They have glow-in-the-dark spots around their mouths that seem to lure plankton and small fish.

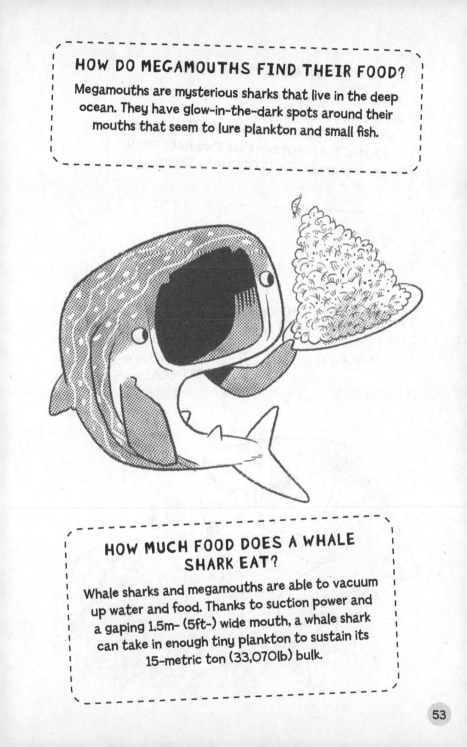

HOW MUCH FOOD DOES A WHALE SHARK EAT?

Whale sharks and megamouths are able to vacuum up water and food. Thanks to suction power and a gaping 1.5m- (5ft-) wide mouth, a whale shark can take in enough tiny plankton to sustain its 15-metric ton (33,070lb) bulk.

DO SHARKS MIGRATE?

Yes, some do. Female blue sharks feed and mate off the east coast of North America, then travel across the Atlantic to give birth off the coast of Africa. The round trip that they make every three years or so is 15,000km (9,321 miles).

WHY DO TIGERS SHARKS GO FOR DINNER IN HAWAII?

Tiger sharks travel to take advantage of gluts of easy prey. The sharks arrive in the waters around Hawaii just as the albatross chicks hatch, then they continue onward to eastern Australia in time for the turtle season.

WHAT IS THE OLDEST SHARK?

Greenland sharks, which live in icy waters near the Arctic Circle, can live for hundreds of years. One shark, identified in 2016, is almost 400 years old!

DID YOU KNOW?

In just one year, lemon sharks grow more than 24,000 new teeth. That's a full set every two weeks! Who needs to bother with brushing?

WHY DO HAMMERHEAD SHARKS LOOK SO ODD?

Hammerhead sharks have wide, hammer-shaped heads with eyes on the tips. Swinging their heads from side to side gives them brilliant all-round vision. During the day, hammerheads often rest together in large groups of up to 100.

WHAT EATS SHARKS?

Sharks are apex predators, which means that they have no natural predators of their own. However, sharks are still at risk from being eaten—by other, bigger sharks!

DO CARPET SHARKS LIVE ON FLOORS?

Some sharks have mottled markings that look like carpet patterns and help camouflage them. The tasselled wobbegong is one of the strangest carpet sharks. Its seaweed-like tentacles swish in the current, disguising the shark and attracting prey.

WHAT IS A SAW SHARK?

Saw sharks are extremely rare. They have wide, flat bodies, but their distinguishing feature is a long, narrow snout studded with pointy teeth. The sharks use this "saw" to slash at fish or to probe the seabed for shellfish.

HOW DO GREAT WHITE SHARKS CATCH THEIR PREY?

Great whites sneak up on their prey from below, swimming up very fast to snatch the unsuspecting creature in their jaws.

DO WHALE SHARKS CARRY PASSENGERS?

Whale sharks don't just feed themselves—they feed hangers-on, too. Remoras are small fish that use suckers on their heads to fix themselves to whale sharks' bellies. They eat scraps that fall from the mouths of their hosts.

WERE THERE SHARKS IN THE AGE OF THE DINOSAUR?

Yes—and long before then, too. Ancestors of the shark were swimming in the world's oceans 450 million years ago, 230 million years before the first dinosaurs appeared.

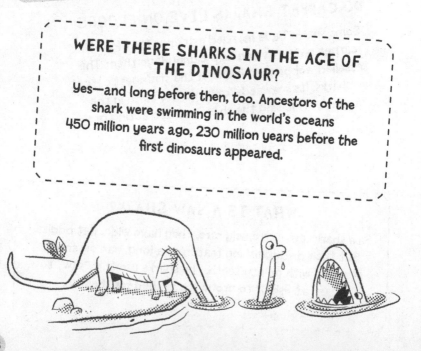

DEEPLY DIPPY

WHAT HAPPENS WHEN AN OCTOPUS LOSES AN ARM?

If an octopus loses an arm, it can grow a new one! Even after it has been cut off, an octopus arm will carry on wriggling for some time.

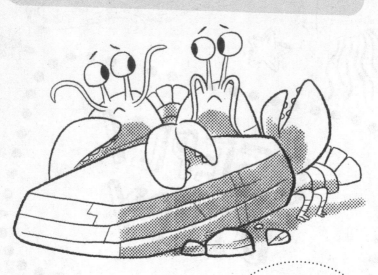

DID YOU KNOW?

An octopus will sometimes eat its own arms, and even its own body, if it becomes extremely stressed.

WHAT ARE LOBSTERS AFRAID OF?

Lobsters are scared of octopuses. Even the sight of one is enough to make a lobster freeze in horror.

HOW BIG IS A BABY OCTOPUS?

When a baby octopus is born, it is about the size of a flea.

DID YOU KNOW?

Some types of octopus contain a poison that instantly kills any creature that eats them.

DOES AN OCTOPUS HAVE MORE THAN ONE HEART?

Octopuses have three hearts! Two pump blood through its gills to help it breathe while the third pumps blood around the rest of its body.

CAN OCTOPUSES CHANGE SHAPE?

The mimic octopus can change its shape and shade in order to scare off predators. It has been known to make itself look like a very convincing sea snake.

DID YOU KNOW?

Octopuses have been known to remove the stinging tentacles from jellyfish and use them as weapons.

WHICH SEA CREATURE HAS THE LARGEST EYES?

The vampire squid has the largest eyes of any animal in relation to its body size. If it was the size of a human, it would have eyes the size of table tennis paddles!

WHY DID DENTISTS LIKE STINGRAYS?

Ancient Greek dentists used the venom from stingrays' spines as an anesthetic.

DID YOU KNOW?

Sharks and rays are the only animals on the planet that are immune to cancer. Scientists believe this may be something to do with their skeletons, which are made of cartilage rather than bone.

HOW DOES A STINGRAY'S STING WORK?

A special cap on the end of a stingray's tail will break off when it attacks its prey. This allows even more poison to flow into its victim's wound.

HOW BIG CAN SQUID GROW?

The largest giant squid ever caught was a whopping 13m (43ft) long and weighed almost a metric ton (2,200lb). Its body was so enormous that calamari rings (squid rings) made from it would have been the size of truck tires!

DID YOU KNOW?

Instead of black ink, some species of deep sea squid squirt a cloud of glowing luminous ink to distract predators in the dark depths of the ocean.

WHY DO LEATHERBACK TURTLES HAVE SPINY THROATS?

The spines keep their meals from escaping! They stop their preferred snack of jellyfish from sliding back out of their mouths.

DID YOU KNOW?

The jaws of a snapping turtle are so powerful that they can rip off a human finger.

HOW LONG CAN TURTLES DIVE FOR?

Green sea turtles can stay underwater for up to five hours. To achieve this, they slow their heart rate to help conserve oxygen, with up to nine minutes between heartbeats.

WHY SHOULD TURTLES AVOID MAN O' WAR JELLYFISH?

When a turtle eats a Portuguese man o' war jellyfish, the jellyfish releases a smell that attracts sharks. It's the jellyfish's way of getting revenge on the turtle!

DID YOU KNOW?

The pistol shrimp got its name from the loud banging noise it makes with its claws in order to surprise its prey.

IS THERE AN ANIMAL WITH JUST ONE EYE?

The only creature known to have just one eye is the copepod. It is a tiny crustacean that swims around in groups of up to one trillion members.

HOW DID THE ROBBER CRAB GET ITS NAME?

The robber crab got its nickname from its habit of stealing shiny things like pots and pans from people's houses! The crab is the largest and heaviest land-living crustacean, weighing up to 4.1kg (9lb). Only the females enter the sea to lay their eggs. If they stay too long, though, they drown!

WHERE CAN YOU FIND MONSTER CRABS?

The Barents Sea is teeming with monster Kamchatka crabs after they were introduced in the 1960s to provide a fishing source for Russian fishermen. The gigantic crustaceans can measure more than 1m (3ft) from claw to claw.

ARE PREHISTORIC CRABS STILL ALIVE TODAY?

Horseshoe crabs are "living fossils." They first appeared on Earth in the Carboniferous period, 300–355 million years ago. Little has changed about their appearance since then, as fossils from the late Jurassic era show.

WHAT IS THE LARGEST CRAB IN THE WORLD?

The largest of all crustaceans is the Japanese spider crab. Its body is about 37cm (15in) across but its legs are like stilts, spanning up to 3.81m (12.5ft).

WHAT IS THE WORLD'S HEAVIEST CRUSTACEAN?

The North Atlantic lobster grows up to 60cm (24in) long and can weigh up to 20kg (44lb), making it the heaviest crustacean that lives in the sea.

WHICH CRUSTACEAN IS THE FASTEST SWIMMER?

While lobsters can leap away from predators at great speed, the fastest-swimming crustacean is Henslow's great swimming crab. Most crabs catch prey by walking up to it but Henslow's crab swims after food at about 4.7km/h (2.9mph).

DID YOU KNOW?

When spiny lobsters migrate, as many as 60 individuals walk in single file along the sea bed. The wandering lobsters can travel 50km (30 miles) without a break.

IS THERE A CRUSTACEAN THAT EXPLODES?

The female fish louse—a tiny crustacean—can give birth to up to 100 babies, but she can't fit them inside her body! As the babies grow, she loses her internal organs to make space for them. When the babies are big enough, the mother explodes, releasing her young but, of course, the mother dies when this happens.

DID YOU KNOW?

The total weight of all the krill (shrimplike crustaceans) in the Antarctic is more than the total weight of all the humans on the planet.

HOW LONG CAN JELLYFISH TENTACLES GROW?

The tentacles of a lion's mane jellyfish can reach up to 36m (120ft) away from its body.

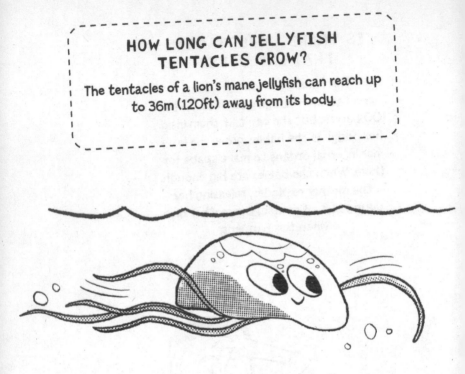

HOW BIG IS THE WORLD'S BIGGEST JELLYFISH?

The largest jellyfish in the world is the Arctic lion's mane that lives in the northwest Atlantic Ocean. Its bell, or body, grows up to 2.1m (7ft) across with tentacles stretching 36.5m (120ft).

CAN JELLYFISH SWIM?

Unlike other jellyfishes, the stinging box jellyfish has many eyes, plus muscles that it uses to swim against the tide, to catch prey—and swimmers!—unaware.

WHAT IS THE DEADLIEST JELLYFISH?

The tentacles of the deadly box jellyfish contain thousands of tiny harpoons, which inject poison into its unlucky victim. The jellyfish's body is about the size of a football, but it's the long tentacles you have to watch out for. There can be up to 60 of them, each up to 4.6m (15ft) long. These are covered with millions of venom-packed capsules. Just 3m (10ft) of tentacle wrapped around a human can deliver a fatal dose.

HOW MANY PEOPLE HAVE DIED FROM BOX JELLYFISH STINGS?

In the waters around Australia, more folks have died from box jellyfish stings than shark or crocodile attacks—about 70 people in the last century. Luckily, an antivenom was developed in 1970.

WHAT IS A JELLYFISH MADE OF?

A jellyfish is 95 percent water—the same as a cucumber! Not as nice in a salad though!

WHAT DO YOU CALL A GROUP OF JELLYFISH?

A group of jellyfish is called a "smack."

DID YOU KNOW?

If you spread them out, the tentacles of an Arctic jellyfish would stretch over 15 tennis courts.

HOW LONG IS A MORAY EEL?

The slender giant moray eel has been known to grow to nearly 4.5m (15ft) in length.

DID YOU KNOW?

The moray eel has two sets of teeth in its throat; the first set bites the eel's prey, while the second set moves up into the eel's mouth and locks on more tightly. The first set then moves to pull the prey down the eel's throat.

HOW DO YOU ESCAPE A MORAY EEL?

If you're bitten by a moray eel, the only way to get away is to kill it by cutting off its head and breaking its jaws. It won't let go while it's alive.

HOW SHOCKING IS AN ELECTRIC EEL?

Electric eels can deliver a shock of 500 volts to stun their prey into submission. The electricity supplied to your home is only 240 volts! You could power two fridges with the electricity produced by a single electric eel.

DID YOU KNOW?

The lamprey, an eel-like creature, has no jaws. To eat, it attaches its sucker mouth to another fish then literally sucks all the fluids out of it, killing the fish by sucking it dry.

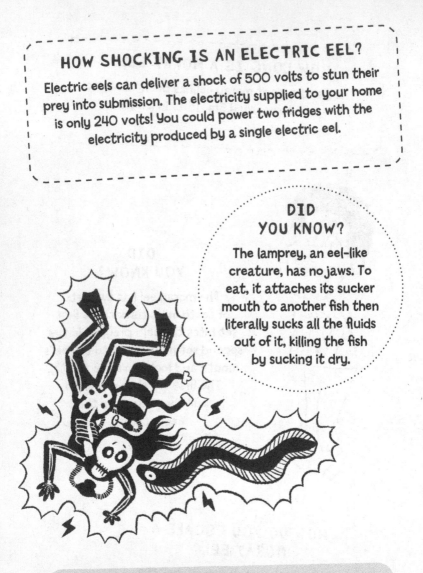

CAN EELS CLIMB UP WALLS?

Glass eels are always determined to get to their destination and have been known to climb up the wet walls of dams to get around an obstacle in their way.

HOW BRAINY IS A SEA STAR?

A sea star doesn't have a brain. An extremely complex nerve system called the nerve plexus controls its arms instead.

$$(f+g)(x) = f(x) + g(x)$$
$$(f-g)(x) = f(x) - g(x)$$
$$(f \times g)(x) = f(x) \, g(x)$$
$$\left[\frac{f}{g}\right](x) = \frac{f(x)}{g(x)} \cdots$$

HOW DOES A SEA STAR EAT?

A sea star can turn its stomach inside out by pushing it through its mouth.

DID YOU KNOW?

Giant sea stars are starfish that can have an arm span of more than 60cm (24in). They can be brown, green, red, or orange.

WHAT IS A MANATEE'S CLOSEST RELATIVE?

The closest living relatives to the manatee are actually elephants and hyrax.

HOW DO WALRUSES SLEEP IN THE SEA?

Walruses fill an inflatable throat pouch called a pharyngeal with air to keep them afloat while they sleep.

DID YOU KNOW?

Odobenus rosmarus, the scientific name for a walrus, is Latin for "tooth-walking sea-horse."

IS THERE A SEA UNICORN?

The long horn of the narwhal is actually an extended tooth! Its other name, "unicorn of the sea," isn't really correct, because it has no horn!

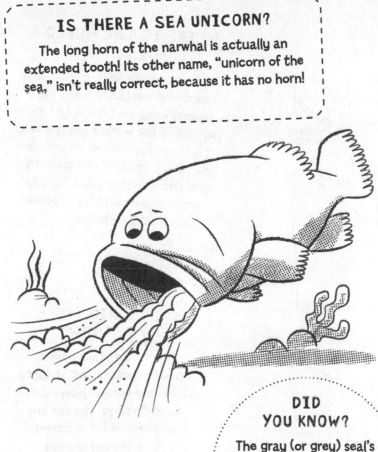

DID YOU KNOW?

The gray (or grey) seal's scientific name, Halichoerus grypus, comes from the Greek meaning "hook-nosed sea pig."

WHICH FISH IS LIKE A VACUUM CLEANER?

Some grouper fish are so huge that when they open their mouths they create a suction that pulls prey straight into their gaping maws.

WHERE IS THE WORLD'S LARGEST REEF?

The Great Barrier Reef, off the east coast of Australia, is the world's largest coral reef, home to five percent of the world's fish species. It is the biggest single structure made by animals. It was created over thousands of years by tiny animals called coral that form a rocky skeleton.

DID YOU KNOW?

When parrotfish munch on hard coral to get at tasty algae, the coral is pooped out as white sand. The fish are responsible for dumping tons of sand around reefs every year.

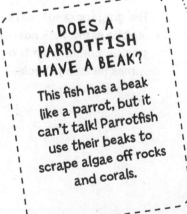

DOES A PARROTFISH HAVE A BEAK?

This fish has a beak like a parrot, but it can't talk! Parrotfish use their beaks to scrape algae off rocks and corals.

WHY SHOULD DIVERS WATCH WHERE THEY STEP?

Is it a piece of weed-covered rock or a fish? Stonefish are disguised to look like stones lying on the seabed. This camouflage hides them from prey and predators, such as bottom-feeding sharks and rays.

ARE STONEFISH DANGEROUS?

Stonefish have a row of needle-like spines on their back that can inject deadly venom. Stonefish venom can kill a person within two hours—unless he or she is treated in time with antivenom.

WHICH FISH WRESTLES WITH ITS MOUTH?

Jawfish have outsized jaws. They fight one another in mouth-wrestling competitions.

HOW DOES A JAWFISH LOOK AFTER ITS EGGS?

Jawfish are mouth brooders. They look after their eggs inside their mouths until they hatch.

DID YOU KNOW?

The jawfish also tunnels with its mouth. It scoops up a mouthful of sand and transports it elsewhere, gradually hollowing out a home.

WHICH FISH MAKES ITS OWN ANTIFREEZE?

The Arctic cod can survive in waters around the north pole that would otherwise turn them to ice cubes. They create an antifreeze protein in their bodies that stops ice crystals from forming in their blood so it stays liquid.

DOES A SWORDFISH SPEAR ITS PREY?

Swordfish have long, pointed bills that look like swords. While prey could get caught on its tip, the swordfish could never reach it with its jaws. It uses the "sword" to slash and injure its prey before grabbing it in its teeth.

IS THERE A DEADLY SNAIL IN THE SEA?

Yes! The cone snail, which lives in the waters of the Indo-Pacific, is a venomous gastropod that injects venom using a disposable dart. The geographer cone is the deadliest cone snail. The venom can cause nausea, dizziness, and sometimes paralysis and death!

CAN DIVERS GET TRAPPED UNDERWATER BY GIANT CLAMS?

Not really. Many adventure movies show divers getting a leg trapped in the closing shell of a giant clam but, while you could fit a leg in some huge bivalve specimens, they close their shells so slowly that most sensible divers could retract a limb before it gets stuck. Which begs the question—what were you doing sticking a leg in a giant clam?!

HOW FAST DO GIANT CLAMS GROW?

Not very fast at all. One North Atlantic deep-sea clam studied by Yale University scientists was estimated to take 100 years to grow about 8mm (0.3in)!

DID YOU KNOW?

The crevalle jack (a type of fish) is capable of producing croaking sounds by grinding its teeth together while releasing gas from its swim bladder.

DO ALL OYSTERS HIDE PEARLS?

No. True natural, round pearls are very rare, as they are created by accident. Most pearls sold in shops are grown in specialized pearl-oyster farms.

HOW BIG WAS THE BIGGEST NATURAL PEARL?

The largest pearl found in the wild was discovered in a giant clam off the coast of Palawan in the Philippines in 1934. The "Pearl of Lao Tzu" weighed 6.4kg (14lb 2oz) and measured 24.1cm (9.5 in) across. It sold at auction in 1980 for $200,000.

HOW ARE PEARLS MADE?

When a pearl oyster senses a parasite or irritant in its shell, it forms a sac around it as a defense. Minerals form around the sac to create a coating of shiny nacre, or mother-of-pearl.

ARE SPONGES ANIMAL OR PLANTS?

Sponges are animals, very primitive ones, that attach themselves to the sea floor. Sponges have many cells, but don't have any organs. They draw water into their bodies through pores and filter it for food and oxygen.

HOW ANCIENT ARE SPONGES?

Sponges were the first many-celled organisms to appear on Earth about 570 million years ago. So, quite ancient, then.

CAN SPONGES GROW FROM BROKEN PIECES OF THEIR BODY?

Yes. A sponge can regenerate from a tiny piece of itself. If you pushed a sponge through a sieve, the individual parts could float away and grow into new sponges.

CAN SEA STARS GROW NEW ARMS?

Yes. All sea stars can grow a new arm if one is lost or bitten off. Some can even grow half their body back, with the two parts regenerating into two separate sea stars!

CAN A SEA STAR GROW BACK FROM A TINY PIECE?

One amazing sea star, in the family Ophidiasteridae, can grow a new body from just a 1cm (0.38in) piece of arm. It can take a year for this to happen, though.

WHY ARE SEA STARS RUINING REEFS?

Spiny sea stars called crown-of-thorns are gobbling up coral reefs. These large, crawling creatures, up to 60cm (24in) across, can eat through half their size in coral in an evening. Large groups of them have been munching on the Great Barrier Reef and reefs in the Red Sea, Indian Ocean, and Pacific. Their spines also contain venom, so they are not easy to get rid of.

DARKEST DEPTHS

WHICH FISH CAN EAT PREY BIGGER THAN ITSELF?

The deep sea gulper eel can open its mouth so wide that its jaws can bend back at a 180-degree angle. This allows it to eat fish larger than itself.

DID YOU KNOW?

If pulled out of the sea by fishermen, the quick change in water pressure makes the gases inside a Pacific grenadier fish expand. Its stomach pops out of its mouth as a result!

HOW DOES A VIPERFISH CATCH ITS PREY?

The viperfish catches its prey by swimming straight toward its target and spearing it on its long teeth.

HOW DOES A VIPERFISH DEAL WITH A BIG MEAL?

The viperfish can move all of its internal organs toward its tail when it needs to make room for a large meal, with its stomach stretching to twice its normal size.

DID YOU KNOW?

Some creatures thrive in the most inhospitable places. In the darkness of the deep ocean, colonies of Pompeii worms live on boiling-hot volcanic vents, like steaming chimneys on the sea bed. Named after the site of a disastrous volcanic eruption in ancient Rome, the worms build crusty tubes to live in and poke their heads out to feed on bacteria.

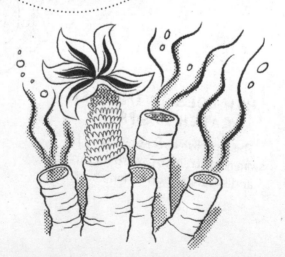

WHICH FISH CARRIES ITS OWN LAMP?

The anglerfish lives in the darkest depths of the sea and has a glowing blob, like a little lantern, dangling in front of its head! The deep-sea anglerfish's lure glows in the dark, so it can be seen through the gloom and tempt prey to come near.

HOW ATTACHED ARE MALE ANGLERFISH TO THEIR MATES?

Some male anglerfish live like parasites on the body of a much bigger female. She may carry as many as six males at a time.

WHICH IS THE GROSSEST FISH OF ALL?

Read on at your own peril—you have been warned! The slime eel, also known as the hagfish, feeds on dead and dying fish at the bottom of the sea. It has a circular mouth full of tiny, triangular teeth. After slipping through a dead creature's mouth, or eye socket, the eel eats the insides of the creature, leaving only a bag of skin and bones behind.

DID YOU KNOW?

When under attack, a hagfish produces slimy mucus, which makes the water around it turn into jelly that is impossible for predators to swim through.

CAN FISH GLOW IN THE DARK?

Some fish live so deep in the sea that sunlight can't reach them and they swim in complete darkness. Many species make their own light using a chemical reaction called bioluminescence.

WHICH FISH HAS TEETH TOO BIG FOR ITS MOUTH?

Thanks to its long, needlesharp teeth, the fangtooth is one of the fiercest-looking fish in the deepest parts of the ocean. When it shuts its mouth, the fangtooth stores its longest lower fangs in two special sockets on either side of its brain.

HOW LAZY IS A BLOBFISH?

The blobfish doesn't move much. Instead it sits and waits for its food to drift by. This 30cm (12in) fish lives in deep waters off Australia. It eats pretty much any small morsel that floats by.

CAN YOU EAT BLOBFISH?

Scientists don't know much about the blobfish—except that it's under threat. It's inedible but trawlers net it while fishing for crabs and lobsters.

DO BLOBFISH FLOAT?

The blobfish's jelly-like flesh is slightly lighter than water. This means the fish can float just above the seabed without expending any energy.

WHERE IS THE DEEPEST PART OF THE SEA?

The Mariana Trench in the western Pacific Ocean is the deepest area of the world's seas. Its maximum depth is 10.98km (6.83 miles). If you placed Mount Everest there, its peak would still be over 2km (6,561ft) below sea level.

HAS ANYONE EVER BEEN THERE?

Only three people have ever dived that deep. The first dive was in the US Navy bathyscaphe Trieste in 1960, with Don Walsh and Jacques Piccard aboard. In 2012 the Canadian movie director James Cameron made the trip in the submersible Deepsea Challenger.

HOW EASY IS IT TO GET TO THE BOTTOM OF THE MARIANA TRENCH?

The pressure at such a depth is enormous, about 1,000 times the atmospheric pressure at sea level, and the temperature just above freezing. The Deepsea Challenger submersible needed steel walls 64mm (2.5in) thick to hold it together and keep the pressure constant for its pilot. The journey to the bottom of the trench took two hours and 37 minutes.

CAN ANY SEA CREATURES SURVIVE IN THE MARIANA TRENCH?

Surprisingly, yes. Divers and remotely controlled underwater vehicles have spotted snailfish near the bottom and what could have been a sea cucumber.

WHICH SEA CREATURE HAS THE BEST NIGHT VISION?

The Gigantocypris is a deep-sea crustacean with a round body made of 95 percent water. It appears more like a jellyfish than other crustaceans, such as crabs or shrimp. The Gigantocypris can see in the darkness at the bottom of the sea thanks to a pair of parabolic mirrors that reflect what little light there is back to its retinas. Despite this adaptation, the images the Gigantocypris sees are probably quite blurred.

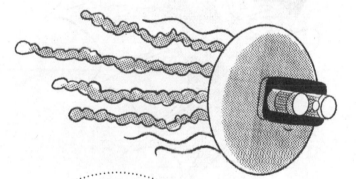

DID YOU KNOW?

The pelican eel is a deep-sea weirdo. It's named for its elastic mouth, which resembles a pelican's stretchy throat. The fish's gaping mouth is about 25cm (10in) long. The rest of its body is snakelike.

ARE THERE DRAGONS IN THE DEEPEST OCEANS?

There is a very spooky creature called the Pacific blackdragon. This 38cm (15in) predator has a snakelike body lit up by photophores on its belly. It waves a small lure from its lower jaw, and when prey comes near, it opens its mouth to reveal a ring of long, sharp fangs. The blackdragon is black on the inside too, so if it swallows luminous fish, they don't glow through its belly!

IS THERE REALLY A VAMPIRE SQUID FROM HELL?

Yes, kinda. A tiny, red creature that looks like a squid with webbing between its arms and glowing eyes has been filmed swimming in the deepest oceans. Commonly known as a vampire squid, its Latin name Vampyroteuthis infernalis does translate as "vampire squid from hell"!

SOMETHING'S FISHY

WHAT IS THE WORLD'S LARGEST BONY FISH?

The ocean sunfish is no beauty, but it is the world's heaviest bony fish. It starts life the size of a sesame seed, but eventually weighs about 1,000kg (1 ton).

HOW MANY EGGS DOES AN OCEAN SUNFISH PRODUCE?

Ocean sunfish females produce more eggs than any other vertebrate—as many as 300 million at a time! How would you like that many brothers and sisters?

WHY IS IT CALLED A SUNFISH?

The sunfish is named for its habit of "sunbathing" at the surface. It may do this to encourage seagulls to land and pick off parasites!

HOW FAST ARE SEAHORSES?

Seahorses are no good for racing, unlike horses on land. With only a small dorsal fin to flutter and push it along, it can take half an hour for a seahorse to swim the length of a human arm.

DO MALE SEAHORSES GET PREGNANT?

Yes! The babies grow for three weeks in a pouch before the male gives birth to up to 200 of them over 72 hours. The effort leaves him looking drained—unsurprisingly!

DID YOU KNOW?

Seahorses can see in two directions at once, as their eyes can move independently of each other.

CAN FISH WALK?

The rosy-lipped batfish isn't a good swimmer, but has modified fins that allow it to walk across the seabed. They make it look like it has legs! The fish has red "lipstick" that helps other rosy-lipped batfish recognize it at spawning time.

DID YOU KNOW?

Unlike other fish, a seahorse swims in an upright position. It also has no scales.

HOW DO ROSY-LIPPED BATFISH HUNT?

The batfish has a lure of frilly flesh on its forehead that tempts prey close enough to eat.

WHAT DO PARROTFISH WEAR AT NIGHT?

At night, parrotfish wrap up their body in a coating of mucus. Scientists think it makes them more difficult for eels and other hunters to sniff out and helps keep parasites away.

HOW DO FROGFISH HIDE FROM PREDATORS?

Frogfish live in warm, shallow seas. Some can change shade to match their surroundings. Some blend in with the seabed and others with their bright coral-reef surroundings.

DO FROGFISH LEAP?

No, but frogfish have leg-like pectoral fins. They use these to crawl slowly across the seabed.

WHAT ARE THE STRANGEST FROGFISH?

The hairy frogfish is a shaggy-looking beast. It feeds on flounders and other flatfish. Another, called the psychedelic frogfish, was discovered off the coast of Indonesia in 2008. Its pattern matches the stripy corals where it lives.

WHICH FISH IS THE MOST VENOMOUS?

The Indian stonefish is said to be the most venomous fish. Easy to mistake for a rock, this camouflaged creature has spines that inflict extremely painful wounds, even through a beach shoe. The effect of being injected by this fish's venom is often fatal.

ARE THERE ANY VENOMOUS SHARKS?

You would think sharks would be scary enough, with their jaws full of jagged teeth, but two species are venomous too! The spiny dogfish and Port Jackson shark are both quite small, at 1.5m (5ft), but they have venomous spines on the front of their dorsal fins.

ARE ANEMONES PLANTS OR ANIMALS?

Sea anemones are predatory animals related to corals and jellyfish. They attach themselves to a reef with a sticky foot, then filter the water with a ring of tentacles. The tentacles hide stinging cells that can paralyze small fish or crabs before they drag the food into their mouth.

WHY DO CLOWNFISH LIVE INSIDE ANEMONES?

Clownfish are immune to anemone toxin so they can use the anemone as a safe location to lay eggs. The clownfish also feed on scraps of food left by the anemone.

WHAT DO ANEMONES GAIN FROM THIS RELATIONSHIP?

Clownfish help protect the anemone from predators. Anemones can also feed on the clownfish's poop!

HOW DOES A PUFFERFISH DEFEND ITSELF?

Pufferfish can puff up like a balloon. This defense makes them too much of a mouthful for most predators—especially since many species are covered in prickles. Oh, and they're poisonous, too!

CAN YOU EAT PUFFERFISH?

In Japan, the poisonous flesh of the pufferfish—fugu—is a delicacy. Only trained chefs can prepare it.

HOW DO PUFFERFISH CATCH THEIR PREY?

Pufferfish rely on sight to find their food. They can move each eye independently.

WHAT IS THE WORLD'S LONGEST BONY FISH?

The four species of oarfish are true monsters of the deep. The giant oarfish is the world's longest bony fish. It usually grows to about 9m (30ft), but there have been reports of fish as long as 17m (55ft).

DO OARFISH COME TO THE SURFACE?

Very rarely. They don't have strong muscles and struggle to survive in choppy waters and strong currents near the surface.

WHERE CAN YOU FIND OARFISH?

Oarfish spend most of their time in deep water. They sometimes swim in an upright pose.

IS THERE A FISH THAT CAN BREATHE ON LAND AND IN WATER?

Most fish soon die if they are taken out of the water—but not the mudskipper. It can breathe on land as well as under water.

HOW DO MUDSKIPPERS BREATHE AIR?

Mudskippers take in oxygen from the air through their skin. They also save bubbles of air in their gills.

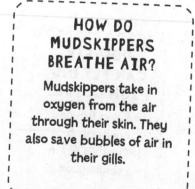

WHERE DO MUDSKIPPERS LIVE?

Mudskippers live in coastal regions. When the tide goes out, they walk or skip around the mud flats looking for food.

DO FLYING FISH ACTUALLY FLY?

Flying fish have a neat trick for escaping marine predators—they leave the water! Swimming at top speed, the fish can break the surface and glide through the air.

WHAT DO FLYING FISH USE FOR WINGS?

The fish glide on stiff, outstretched pectoral fins. Their average gliding speed is about 16km (10 miles) per hour.

HOW FAR CAN FLYING FISH GLIDE?

A flying fish can cover up to 180m (590ft) in a single glide.

ARE ANY PREHISTORIC FISH STILL ALIVE?

For a long time scientists only knew about coelacanths from fossils. They thought they had become extinct millions of years ago. But then in 1938 a live coelacanth was caught!

DID YOU KNOW?

If you kept a goldfish in a darkened room for long enough, it would eventually turn white.

HOW LONG IS A COELACANTH PREGNANCY?

Coelacanth eggs develop inside the mother's body perhaps for as long as three years. Then, the mother gives birth to five or more well-developed young.

DO ANY FISH LIVE IN MUD?

A killifish embryo can survive in mud, with no water or oxygen, for more than 60 days.

COULD FISH SURVIVE IN A TANK OF HUMAN BLOOD?

Most tropical marine fish could survive in a tank filled with human blood due to the amount of oxygen it contains.

HOW MANY DIFFERENT KINDS OF FISH ARE THERE?

So far, around 32,000 species of fish have been identified, compared with only 6,400 species of mammal.

WHERE DO MOST OF THE FISH LIVE?

Less than 0.1 percent of Earth's water is fresh water, yet it is home to a whopping 40 percent of all fish species.

DID YOU KNOW?

When fully grown, the Philippine goby fish is only 0.7cm (0.3in) long. That's smaller than your little fingernail!

WHAT IS THE MOST TOXIC THING IN THE SEA?

The most toxic natural poison in the world comes from a piece of coral. The poison of the Palythoa can kill a rabbit with only a 25-nanogram injection; 4 micrograms can kill a human. Death occurs within minutes and there is no known antidote.

DID YOU KNOW?

When it has eaten as much as it can, a barracuda will herd any remaining fish that it has not eaten into shallow water. It guards them until it is ready to eat again.

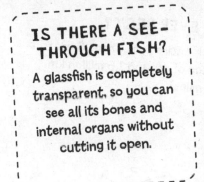

DO TUNA FISH EVER REST?

Tuna fish swim constantly for their entire lives. Over 15 years, a single tuna will cover a distance of around 1.6 million km (1 million miles).

WHAT DOES A BARRACUDA EAT FOR ITS LAST MEAL?

A dying barracuda fish will gorge itself on anything that will make its flesh poisonous, such as small creatures and plants. That way, anything that eats the barracuda after it dies will also be killed. Nasty!

DID YOU KNOW?

Some fish can get seasick.

HOW MANY EGGS DOES A COD LAY?

A female cod can lay up to nine million eggs in a single pregnancy.

WHICH FISH HAS TEETH ON ITS TONGUE?

Lizardfish are bottom-dwelling fish with a mouth full of sharp teeth, even on their tongues!

WHY ARE CATFISH EXTRA TASTY?

A catfish has ten times as many taste buds as a human.

CAN FISH SURVIVE IN VERY SALTY WATER?

The desert pupfish, found in isolated pools in Death Valley, USA, can survive in water three times saltier than the ocean. It can also endure temperatures of more than 38°C (100°F).

WHAT'S THE OLDEST ANIMAL EVER FOUND?

A quahog clam found off the coast of Iceland in 2007 has been identified as being between 405 and 410 years old, making it the oldest animal ever discovered. It was a baby when Elizabeth I was on the throne in England (1558–1603), and was nearly 350 years old by the end of World War II!

WHICH FISH CAN GET A JOB IN A HEALTH SPA?

Some health spas use garra rufa fish to treat skin problems. People sit in shallow pools filled with the fish, then wait for their dead skin and scabs to be nibbled away!

WHY SHOULD YOU NEVER WALK A DOG NEAR A CERTAIN GERMAN LAKE?

In 2001, a giant catfish in a park lake in Germany became known as "Kuno the killer" after it jumped out and ate a Dachshund puppy—whole!

DID YOU KNOW?

The flying gurnard swims in water, walks on land, and flies through the air ... and most unbelievable of all, it's a fish!

WHY SHOULDN'T YOU EAT A BLUE TANG?

Despite its beautiful looks, the flesh of the blue tang fish is actually poisonous if eaten by humans or other fish.

HOW BIG CAN CLAMS GROW?

The tridacna clam has been known to grow up to 1.2m (4ft) long and weigh up to 227kg (500lb). Not bad for a clam!

CAN ANY FISH WALK ON DRY LAND?

The Asian climbing perch can "walk" on land in search of water when its water source dries up. It uses its fins and tail to pull itself along the ground.

HOW FAST IS A SAILFISH?

The cosmopolitan sailfish can swim faster than a cheetah can run! It can swim 109km (68 miles) per hour— that's 9km (6 miles) faster than a cheetah's top speed.

DID YOU KNOW?

The sailfish has a dorsal fin along most of its back that can be raised like a sail when it's excited.

WHICH SEA CREATURE HAS 100 EYES?

A scallop has about 100 eyes around the edge of its shell. Very handy for spotting approaching predators!

CAN ANY FISH SURVIVE FOR YEARS OUT OF WATER?

The lungfish can live out of water for as long as four years!

DID YOU KNOW?

A sea slug can eat a hydroid (an underwater stinging nettle) without being stung. The stinging chemical is absorbed into its skin and then stings anything that tries to eat the slug. Clever!

WHAT HAPPENS WHEN YOU PLAY CHESS WITH A SOLE?

If you place a sole (a type of flat fish) on a chessboard, it will take just four minutes to change its skin patterns to match the squares on the board.

CAN FISH CHEW?

Because of the design of their jaws, fish can't actually chew—they swallow most of their food whole.

DID YOU KNOW?

In 2003, the Australian navy boarded an Indonesian ship that was drifting off the coast and found no sign of the crew or indications of an emergency. The only thing they found onboard was 3 metric tons (6,614lb) of rotting mackerel and tuna.

DO ALL FISH HAVE RED BLOOD?

Some fish in Antarctica have a natural antifreeze in their bodies which makes their blood appear white instead of red.

WHO MADE A GLOW-IN-THE-DARK GOLDFISH?

Why keep normal pet goldfish when a Taiwanese company has made a fish that glows in different shades? By injecting a protein extracted from jellyfish, the super-fish glows gold under normal light and a variety of different shades under aquarium lights.

DID YOU KNOW?

The long-nosed chimaera fish lives in the deep sea around South Africa at depths of 2,438m (8,000ft) and has a nose shaped like a fighter plane. Don't get too close, though, as a single touch from its spine is enough to kill a human.

WHY ARE HERRING LIKE SOLDIERS?

The collective name for a group of herring is an army.

WHICH FISH IS A SPITTER?

The archerfish likes to lurk near the surface of the water before spitting well-targeted jets to knock down passing flying insects and eating them. The archerfish can hit prey from a distance of 1.5m (5ft).

IS A LIONFISH DANGEROUS?

The lionfish looks beautiful, with its orange striped patterns and long fins, like feathers, sprouting all over its body, but watch out! The fins and spines on its body are for defense and are highly venomous. A sting from one of these can cause a human diver excruciating pain.

CAN ANY FISH HAVE BABIES WITHOUT PARTNERS?

Some female bony fish can produce babies without a partner. The baby is a clone of its mother.

WHICH FISH TASTES WITH TOUCH?

Catfish have tastebuds on their barbels (fleshy whiskers) which means that they can taste things by simply brushing up against them.

IS THERE A FISH THAT CROAKS?

The black drum (a type of fish found in the Gulf of Mexico) gets its name from its ability to use its large swim bladder to produce croaking or drumming sounds.